When Faith Feels Dry

Rediscovering Joy in God

Caleb Davis

New Growth Press
newgrowthpress.com

New Growth Press, Greensboro, NC 27401
newgrowthpress.com

Cover Design: Dan Stelzer
Interior Typesetting and Ebook: Lisa Parnell,
lparnellbookservices.com

ISBN: 978-1-64507-631-5 (paperback)
ISBN: 978-1-64507-632-2 (ebook)

Library of Congress Cataloging-in-Publication Data on file

Printed in India

30 29 28 27 26 1 2 3 4 5

Skeletons are creepy. These dried-out approximations of a human remind us of what's missing: muscles and skin and *life*. They tell us what used to be there and stand as a symbol of loss. What was once alive is now a shell.

Sometimes our faith feels dry like this. Our walk with God, once joyful and life-giving, can begin to feel empty. Routine. Dehydrated. The structure and shape of our faith are there, but not the spark of life. You may feel this way right now.

You pull into the church parking lot, say hello to a few friends, and find your seat in the sanctuary. You stand for the songs and mouth the words. The sermon starts, and you nod at a few interesting points. You take communion. Say a prayer. You are on autopilot.

Later in the week, you attend small group. The discussion is . . . okay. As you talk about the Bible, you know the words are true. You believe they matter. But they don't land on your heart. You have a couple of moments of prayer during the day, one before dinner, maybe one before bed, but it feels like you are praying more out of habit than anything else. You're trying to do all the right things, but you still feel spiritually dry.

The Disconnect Between Head and Heart

For many of us, feeling spiritually dry isn't due to lack of knowledge. We understand the essentials for a right relationship with God, and we believe the gospel. We agree with Scripture and know that its words are true. The problem is that what we *know* about God doesn't seem to *do* anything for us. There's a palpable disconnect between our heads and our hearts.

We know God loves us, but we don't *feel* it. We know God is in control, but we're still anxious. We know God speaks, but we struggle to hear his voice. We know God is there, but it's easy to go all day without thinking of him. We are still committed to God, but we don't feel close to him.

This isn't what you thought life with God would be like, is it? Maybe you remember a time when your faith felt alive. You sang from your heart, and sermons seemed personal, as if the pastor knew exactly what was happening in your life. The Bible felt like it was written just for you. Serving felt like a privilege, and God's mission excited you. You confessed deeply, rejoiced greatly, and felt the nearness of God. But something changed. And you began to wonder, *Is this really what "abundant life" means? Is this what God wants for me? Is this just my new normal?*

Spiritual dryness feels like a world where all the color has faded away.

The Experience of Dryness Is Not Unusual

If you are struggling with spiritual dryness, please know that many, if not most, Christians have this experience during their life. This emptiness is a common obstacle, whether it originates in severe exhaustion, daily struggles, medical difficulties, or just a monotonous season of life.

Thankfully, we have God's Word to show us that his people have long been wrestling with this same difficulty as they seek to follow the Lord. Throughout the Psalms, we hear the pain of people who know God is there but struggle to experience him. See if these words resonate with your experience:

> I will say to God, my rock,
> "Why have you forgotten me?" (Psalm 42:9)

> God, you are my God; I eagerly seek you.
> I thirst for you;
> my body faints for you
> in a land that is dry, desolate, and without water.
> (Psalm 63:1)

Many of us feel like the writer of these psalms. We wonder why the Bread of Life tastes stale or why our heavenly Father feels like a relative we only see once a year. And because we don't always know how we got to this point, it's hard to find the first step in moving forward.

What God Desires for You

Before we proceed, you need to know that God desires so much more for you. He has gone to great lengths to pour his joy into your life. As you grapple with the discouragement of a dry season, don't panic. God hasn't forgotten about you, and he welcomes you to come to him in any frame of mind or heart you find yourself in. He will help you take steps forward.

The Westminster Catechism says, "Man's chief end is to glorify God, and to enjoy him forever."[1] This is why the Lord created you. He wants you to experience the deepest and most lasting joy imaginable. This isn't a side quest or bonus for the extra-spiritual person. This is the very purpose for which you were made.

From Genesis to Revelation, the Bible declares that God created his people to experience joy—"a good feeling in the soul, produced by the Holy Spirit, as he causes us to see the beauty of Christ."[2] You'll find this theme throughout Scripture:

- In the Lord's presence is "abundant joy" (Psalm 16:11).
- Jesus's birth ushered in "good news of great joy" for all people (Luke 2:10).
- The goal of Jesus's teaching was to invite us into his joy (John 15:11).
- When people receive the gospel, it is accompanied by "great joy" (Acts 8:8).

- The kingdom of God is marked by joy (Romans 14:17).
- The return of Jesus will cause us to overflow with great joy (1 Peter 4:13).

God is the fountain and source of all joy. All that we see of him revealed in his Word is not only to be studied, acknowledged, nor even believed, but most fully *delighted in*. He is committed to giving us true and lasting delight in him. Every part of who he is, what he does, and what he commands is for our good and our soul's satisfaction.

God invites you to know and enjoy him

God's revelation of himself is his invitation. What's more, whatever you have learned about the character of God, there is still more to discover. The Bible doesn't only tell us that God is loving, righteous, gracious, and faithful; it tells us that he is all these things in infinite measure:

- Not just loving, but abounding in steadfast love (Exodus 34:6).
- Not just righteous, but exceedingly righteous (Psalm 71:19).
- Not just gracious, but overflowing in grace (Ephesians 1:7–8).
- Not just faithful, but faithful forever (2 Timothy 2:13).

All of his excellencies are infinite—and they are all intended to be enjoyed. Even now, he invites you to see and enjoy him.

When Jesus met the Samaritan woman at the well, he said, "Whoever drinks from the water that I will give him will never get thirsty again. In fact, the water I will give him will become a well of water springing up in him for eternal life" (John 4:13–14). That's the opposite of dryness. She said, "Sir, give me this water" (John 4:15). Is this what you also want? Why not pause right now and pray this prayer: "Lord, give me this water."

God gives you strength to fight for joy

How does what we know about God become real and alive to us? Here is the key: The joy of the Lord is available to each of us, but it is not given to us automatically. We must fight for and pursue the joy he's made available to his children, remembering that he is with us as we fight.

Have you considered joy something you must fight for? If we're not naturally emotional, we may think we shouldn't expect to feel close to God. But joy is not the same thing as an emotional high. It's not even the same thing as denying our sorrows. The Bible assures us that we may be "grieving, yet always rejoicing" (2 Corinthians 6:10).

Have you thought that fighting for joy is unnecessary—that time will eventually heal the distance in the relationship? We imagine that as soon as our circumstances change, our hearts will change. But usually the greatest fight we have is not the fight against our circumstances—sickness, kids, jobs, finances, marriage, or any other thing—but rather the fight against our very own soul. What's more, the Lord makes joy available to us even in the middle of life's troubles.

Have you been willing to settle for less? Scripture gives us approximately two hundred exhortations to rejoice. This not only means that God clearly wants us to have joy but also that we tend to settle for less. We drift, forget, or reject the deep soul satisfaction available to us. We are prone to miss out on the very thing we want so badly.

Have you been passive? Because life is hard, we are forgetful, and because the enemy presses in on us, we must not presume that spiritual dehydration will just go away on its own. We must take action in order to have joy. This is what we see in Psalm 42. Take a moment and read it in its entirety. The psalmist describes his dryness and his longing for more:

> As a deer longs for flowing streams,
> so I long for you, God.
> I thirst for God, the living God.
> When can I come and appear before God?
> My tears have been my food day and night,
> while all day long people say to me,
> "Where is your God?" (Psalm 42:1–3)

His words are filled with questioning, oppression, and pain. But he doesn't stop there or crumble. The pain is present, but so is his fight. Twice he questions himself,

> Why, my soul, are you so dejected?
> Why are you in such turmoil?
> Put your hope in God, for I will still praise him,
> my Savior and my God. (Psalm 42:5)

Like the psalmist, we must fight our own hearts to remember our joy and hope in God. Jesus didn't die to give you a lifeless, joyless, dry faith—he came to bring abundant life, waters welling up inside of you with the Spirit dwelling in you (John 4:14; 10:10).

However long you have felt dry, however many solutions you have tried, however hopeless you feel right now, do not give up. You can get back to what you were designed for. You are not fighting alone. The Holy Spirit leads and empowers you. God delights to answer these prayers, and you are asking for the very thing he most wants to give.

Ways to Move Forward in Spiritual Dryness

What can you do when you feel spiritually dry? Let's look at seven practical ways to move forward by faith.

1. Engage with God

The reason for spiritual dryness is often simple: We're not drinking. We can't expect to feel alive in our faith when we are barely connected to the source of life. What kind of time are you spending with your heavenly Father?

Life rhythms shift. A newborn arrives, you get sick, jobs change, or you move. Schedules get disrupted. Once shaken up, we can find it hard to get back to the life-giving habits of prayer, Scripture meditation, or study. Sometimes this pause continues for years, and we slowly disengage and drift.

We cannot be satisfied in God if we're not spending time with him. We cannot enjoy him if we're not engaging with him. How do we do this?

Listen to how the apostle John opens his first letter:

> What was from the beginning, what we have heard, what we have seen with our eyes, what we have observed and have touched with our hands, concerning the word of life—that life was revealed, and we have seen it and we testify and declare to you the eternal life that was with the Father and was revealed to us—what we have seen and heard we also declare to you, so that you may also have fellowship with us; and indeed our fellowship is with

> the Father and with his Son, Jesus Christ. We are writing these things so that our joy may be complete. (1:1–4)

John says that during Jesus's time on earth the disciples experienced direct fellowship with him. Imagine how awesome that would be! When facing difficult decisions, they could just walk up to Jesus and ask him about it. Instead of asking for God's comfort, they could just go on a walk with Jesus, eat a meal with him, and receive a hug from him. He could literally calm the storm around them.

John is not trying to make us jealous as he describes these experiences with Jesus. His description is really an invitation: "*so that you may also have fellowship with us*" (v. 3). Jesus is still alive; he still offers fellowship, and he wants to engage with you.

How do we receive this gift? We are able to experience the same joy of fellowship that the first believers had as we read the testimony of the apostles and interact with the living Word of God. John explains at the end of his gospel, "But these [the signs and stories of Jesus] are written so that you may believe that Jesus is the Messiah, the Son of God, and that by believing you may have life in his name" (20:31).

Sometimes when we read a book or watch a movie, we begin to feel like we know the characters, like we are part of the story. We may cry at a main character's death, be inspired by the general's speeches on horseback, or clap at the victory shot in the championship game. Though our emotion is real, our presence with the characters is not.

But the Bible is different from other stories. We actually do enter into the story and into relationship with God as we read the Bible. This is because God's Word isn't just a collection of stories or truths to be studied and applied; it's God speaking, drawing us into fellowship with him. We open the Bible and hear his voice (his promises, correction, character, and work). We respond back to him in prayer (worship, thanksgiving, confession, supplication). Speaking, listening, and responding are all involved. These are the ingredients of all relationships. And this is why we open the Bible. It is more than just reading; it's relating.

Take a moment and reflect. You may want to write answers to the following questions in a journal: Am I listening to the Lord's voice in his Word? Am I responding to him in prayer? Maybe now is the moment to pause and talk to him. Confess ways you have been neglecting or ignoring him. Receive his invitation to come near.

2. Consider your unresolved hurt

If we're honest, one reason we may feel far from God is that we have pulled away emotionally. We asked God for some things that he didn't deliver in the way we thought he would. We prayed about a difficult situation and waited for his guidance, but he seemed silent. Perhaps a season of suffering lingered . . . and lingered. Our hopes and dreams may have been unfulfilled.

Disappointment, discouragement, and disillusionment can turn to doubt. Probably not doubt in God's existence, but maybe doubt in God's goodness. Or perhaps we believe he is good toward others but hasn't been good to us.

When we struggle in this way, we can hear all sorts of truths about God—but we wonder if we really still believe them. We can lose our confidence in his love, wisdom, control, and presence.

The truth is that we cannot trust our emotions. Though we may not understand the way God has arranged our lives, we can trust him because we know that he has given us his Son (Romans 8:31–32). This is the ultimate proof that he is for us. It may be a struggle to understand what he allows into our lives because God's ways are higher than our ways and his thoughts higher than our thoughts (Isaiah 55:8). But trust your Father. Remember who he is. Since he's so committed to you that he paid the ultimate price to rescue you from sin and death, you can rest in the loving care of an infinitely merciful Lord.

How have hurt and disappointment drawn you away from closeness to God? What lies have clouded your vision of him? Come to him with your struggles. Write down a few key promises from Scripture to cling to. Remember and rehearse specific ways that you have seen God show up in your life. Find some songs that help you sing these truths. Let these things reset your heart and draw you back to him.

3. Consider your loves

We can be blind because our eyes are closed, but we can also be blind because our view is overloaded. Think about the *Where's Waldo?* books. What makes this skinny man in a striped shirt so hard to find? It's that he is hidden among pages so filled with clutter that it is easy to miss him.

Perhaps your preoccupation with other things has crowded the pages of your life and made it difficult to see God. Have the cares of this world choked out the seed of faith? The love of comfort, security, health, approval, or success can all fill our hearts. Whether we are stressed as we work toward goals, anxious at the possibility of not achieving them, or are busy enjoying the results of hard work, each of these can tug our hearts away from God. We try many things to satisfy our spiritual thirst, but unless we are drinking from the living water Jesus offers, we are actually taking in saltwater. And the more we take in, the drier we become.

What is the solution to our restless search? Many people would say contentment should be the goal—we need to be grateful for what we have and avoid mindless consumerism. But this is not enough.

Our hearts are hungry. They are aching to be filled. When we try to fill them, they always need more and more. As the unstable pleasures attached to success, approval, and health fade, the joy these things bring also wanes.

What is the cure? Your soul can only be satisfied by the eternal food of God himself. Do you remember these verses?

- Taste and see that the LORD is good. How happy is the person who takes refuge in him! (Psalm 34:8).
- "I am the bread of life," Jesus told them. "No one who comes to me will ever be hungry, and no one who believes in me will ever be thirsty again" (John 6:35).

God doesn't only want you to know that he is good; he wants you to *taste* and experience that he is good. There is a difference between reading a recipe for chocolate chip cookies and actually sinking your teeth into a cookie. God's intention is not just that we know his "ingredients"—his attributes—but that we experience the goodness of who he is.

We can come to the Bible and read it like a book or we can engage with it like a meal. We can savor who God is, noting everything we learn about his character and his ways. Chew on the truths that he is the Creator who set the planets in motion with a word (Psalm 33:6), the trustworthy Redeemer who displays his covenant faithfulness yesterday, today, and forever (Psalm 136), and the loving Father who graciously forgives both the lost prodigals and the self-righteous older brothers (Luke 15:11–32).

Here are some ideas for savoring the goodness of God: Make a list of how you see God's character on display in Scripture. Then consider how you have seen examples of his goodness in your life. Go through each item slowly—perhaps just a few examples a day—so you can really absorb them. Practice praising God for everything you see.

4. Consider your sins

I remember meeting with someone who told me, "I don't feel God's presence anymore. Why don't I feel close to him?" As I asked some questions to better understand what was going on in this man's life, he confessed that he was involved in sexual sin. As kindly as possible, I told him, "God hasn't left you—you've left him."

The Bible often talks about our faith as a walk with God. But we imagine ourselves charting a course and Jesus following along wherever we go. The biblical image is Jesus calling us to join him as he walks (Luke 9:23). This means that when we walk in sin, we are walking in the opposite direction of God. True joy is found only in walking *with* Jesus.

Are you walking in sin? Have you tolerated sexual sin, bitterness, lies, marital neglect, unchecked anger, laziness, or greed in your life? Maybe it started small and snowballed. Maybe you planned to deal with it, but it got out of hand. With each step, you find yourself further and further from where you want to be in your relationship with God and others. The distance grows and the joy fades. And the longer this goes on, the harder it feels to return to God in repentance because guilt and shame hang over you like a cloud.

Sin is always relational. It is not just behaving badly; it is rejecting and ignoring the good God who loves us. Sin leads to guilt, guilt leads to hiding, and hiding leads to more sin. If you are on this destructive path, you need to hear this clearly: You will not have the joy of God while walking in sin. You cannot walk the path of death and expect the joy of life.

But you can always come back. David prayed after his grievous sin: "Restore the joy of your salvation to me" (Psalm 51:12). That prayer can be yours too. If you return to the Lord in repentance, he receives you. Always. He is faithful to forgive (1 John 1:9). He delights to welcome you to walk alongside him again.

Take a moment right now and ask yourself, *Have I tolerated sin in my life? Have I been resisting the Spirit's conviction? What do I need to confess and turn from?*

5. Cultivate a thankful heart

Most marriage counselors will tell couples that one of the main ways they can repair their marriage is to begin tracking and communicating reasons they are grateful for their spouse. This sounds simple, but in a lifelong relationship, people can begin to take the other person for granted. All the gifts, service, time, words, and love that come from one spouse can be easily forgotten or missed by the other.

The same cycle tends to happen between us and God. For most of us, it is simply easier to see the problems around us, both in our lives and in the world. Pain comes into focus more easily than blessings. And when we do see the good in our lives, we can be tempted to view it as our own doing. Most of us have had the experience of praying to God, receiving what we asked for, and then moving on without acknowledging God.

Cultivating thankfulness begins with our asking God to help us see who he is and what he's doing. If we take the time to notice, we will see that "the earth is full of the LORD's unfailing love" (Psalm 33:5). James says, "Every good and perfect gift is from above" (1:17). Every good thing you enjoy—every hobby, every beautiful view, every food, every person, every pleasure that you have ever had—you have because God created it and gave it to you.

Our joy in the Lord increases measurably as we recognize his intentional generosity. If you find $100 on the ground, you have a measure of happiness. But this joy deepens when the $100 comes inside a card from someone you love. Knowing it is given with you in mind multiplies the joy. God wants us to know that he is the Creator; but he also wants us to know that his creations are gifts he gives us out of love.

Consider: What good gifts has God given you that you can thank him for? Take time today to receive his loving gifts. Eat a good meal, laugh with your kids, go on a walk, have fun. Thank God each time he sanctifies the ordinary moments that fill your life (1 Timothy 4:1–5). Then also thank him for the Holy Spirit in your life.

6. Seek help from others

Pursuing joy in God is not something you can do alone. Have you been trying to figure this out by yourself? Have you kept your doubt, discouragement, and dryness hidden from others?

I have seen that as life gets harder, often we pull away from others. We don't feel like we have the energy to engage. Perhaps we're tired of answering questions. Or we expect people to tire of our burdens. But these are exactly the times God wants to care for and encourage us through the help of his people. The Bible presents the church as a body, and just like a body, each part is both needy and needed. We only fully experience what God has for us as we recognize our interdependence on brothers and sisters in Christ.

You need the church. God has given us the Lord's Day to gather together each week and remember who he is and what he has done for us in Jesus. We sing in worship both to praise God and to remind ourselves of what is true. I know that some weeks it's hard to even get in the door. But the consistent power of meeting every week will bring you life. Are you committed to gathering with the body of Christ?

Meeting with the body of Christ includes being honest. People can't help you if they don't know your heart struggles. Tell people about your spiritual dryness. Ask for prayer. Paul often prays for the church to know God more (Ephesians 3:14–21). He doesn't just teach them about God; he prays. That means he believed his prayer would be part of how other believers experienced greater joy and clearer spiritual sight. Ask others to do this with you.

As we share, we need to be open to receiving input from our brothers and sisters in Christ. Give people permission to speak words of correction, encouragement, and counsel (see Galatians 6:2). The Word of God is often more powerful coming from the mouth of others than reading it alone.

Consider: Who can you talk to about your struggle?

7. Look for ways to help others

Christians often think, *I need to be fed. I need a good church with good teaching, good discussions, and studies that feed me. I need more content.*

This might be part of the problem. Maybe you are being fed too much. Maybe you struggle with a consumer mindset, thinking exclusively about what you can get out of your local church rather than what you can give. Instead, think about how you can serve, welcome, and invest in others. Food is meant to be fuel. We have to burn the calories we take in. We are not designed to stuff our face with spiritual food without taking any action. We are meant to hear and obey.

Perhaps your faith feels dry because it is not being used or applied. God has fed you so that you are nourished to love others, be devoted to good works, and serve as a part of the body. And as our faith produces action, our spirits are enriched and enlivened. Serving awakens joy in us, as Proverbs 11:25 describes: "Whoever brings blessing will be enriched, and one who waters will himself be watered" (ESV).

Sometimes our faith feels dry because we live like we don't need it. We don't remember God's provision because we aren't being generous. We don't think about God's protection because we aren't risking anything. We don't feel compelled to ask God for strength because we aren't in situations where we are serving beyond ourselves. We don't need to be reminded of God's faithfulness because we are absorbed in our own comfort.

What happens when you instead put yourself in a position where you remember you need God because you are engaged in consistent, Christlike love and mission? In this place of dependence, you turn to the Lord regularly. And you see him act as he meets you, sustains you, and fills you.

Who is God calling you to serve? What have you been learning that you can teach someone else? What blessings has he given you that can meet someone else's need?

Time to Drink from His Well

When our faith feels dry, it's easy to grasp for quick comforts like food or drink, the distraction of our phones, or even something good such as a vacation or time in nature. These activities are like taking aspirin for a headache caused by dehydration. They may numb the symptoms, but they won't fix the problem.

As hard as it can be to journey through it, spiritual dryness can be a gift because it reveals your soul's thirst and drives you to the true water your soul needs. And the good news is that Jesus has an endless supply of living water available to you.

You do not have to stay where you are. I've watched God bring many people through this struggle. He can do the same for you. This time next year will be different.

Revisit the methods for moving forward that we explored. Consider one each day over the next week. Ask God to meet you as you ponder each factor that may be contributing to this dry season. He is willing, ready, and near to help.

Hear Jesus's life-giving words: "If anyone is thirsty, let him come to me and drink. The one who believes in me, as the Scripture has said, will have streams of living water flow from deep within him" (John 7:37–38).

Today he is crying out to you. Come. Drink.

Endnotes

1. Westminster Assembly, *The Westminster Confession of Faith*, Edinburgh ed. (William S. Young, 1851), 387, https://www.monergism.com/thethreshold/sdg/westminster/The%20Westminster%20Confession%20of%20Faith_New.pdf.

2. John Piper, "How Do You Define Joy?" *desiringGod*, July 25, 2015, https://www.desiringgod.org/articles/how-do-you-define-joy.